Super File-Folder Books

Easy How-to's for 10 Interactive Books That Kids Will Love to Make and Read

by Rozanne Lanczak Williams

NEW YORK • TORONTO • LONDON • AUCKLAND • SYDNEY

MEXICO CITY • NEW DELHI • HONG KONG • BUENOS AIRES

Teaching Resources

To the teachers, staff, and cool kids of
Lee Elementary School, Los Alamitos, California. You rock!
—RLW

Cover design, interior design, and interior photos by Josué Castilleja
Cover photos by Studio 10
Interior illustrations by Maxie Chambliss, except page 6 by Jason Robinson
and dinosaurs on page 26 by Edward Heck

ISBN: 0-439-39502-X
Copyright © 2004 by Rozanne Lanczak Williams
Published by Scholastic Inc.
All rights reserved.
Printed in the U.S.A.

2 3 4 5 6 7 8 9 10   40   11 10 09 08 07 06 05 04

Contents

Introduction...4

What's Inside.......................................5

How to Make File-Folder Books..................6

File-Folder Books

The Wheels on the Bus.........................8

Silly Spiders.....................................12

I Like Books!....................................16

Miss Lucy.......................................20

Ten Little Dinosaurs............................24

All Kinds of Homes.............................28

My Monster Book...............................32

Button Bear.....................................36

Piggy Bank Book................................40

On the Go!......................................44

Book Links......................................48

INTRODUCTION

Dear Teacher,

Welcome to *Super File-Folder Books*! Encourage, inspire, and support the growing literacy skills of your beginning readers with 10 adorable, easy-to-make books using file folders as covers. Simply trace the cover templates onto file folders and cut them out to create sturdy, colorful, and inviting covers in fun shapes—from dinosaurs to piggy banks! Children personalize the reproducible book pages with text and artwork to make the books truly their own.

Enhance your literacy program by including bookmaking activities as part of your classroom routine throughout the school year. Making books with children encourages their interest in writing and helps nurture a lifelong love of reading. After sharing their books at school, young authors will enjoy taking their books home to reread again and again with family members.

Why Make Books?
Bookmaking in the classroom is a great way to
- create age-appropriate books.
- give children practice reading high-frequency words in context.
- introduce children to the steps in the writing process.
- engage children in a meaningful activity during center time or when you are working with small groups.
- integrate reading and writing into the content areas with books that reinforce math skills (*Ten Little Dinosaurs*, *Piggy Bank Book*) and science concepts (*All Kinds of Homes*).
- create a supply of reading material for children to take home.

Have fun making, reading, and sharing file-folder books!

Rozanne Lanczak Williams

Rozanne Lanczak Williams

Connections to the Language Arts Standards

The activities in this book support the following language arts standards, outlined by Mid-continent Research for Education and Learning (McREL), a nationally recognized nonprofit organization that collects and synthesizes national and state K–12 standards.

* Uses the stylistic and rhetorical aspects of writing.

* Uses grammatical and mechanical conventions in written compositions.

* Uses the general skills and strategies of the reading process.

Source:
Content Knowledge: A Compendium of Standards and Benchmarks for K–12 Education, 4th edition (Mid-continent Research for Education and Learning)

WHAT'S INSIDE

For each file-folder book, you'll find the following:

Directions for the Teacher
This page includes:
- a sample of a completed book cover and an interior page.
- a list of materials.
- easy step-by-step directions for making the cover and completing the interior pages. (Note: The directions and materials lists given are for making only one book. Multiply accordingly for the number of books you plan to make.)
- quick writing activities such as variations on the file-folder book and extension activities.

Cover Template
Each template is a simple and appealing shape that ties in to popular primary themes.

Book Pages
Each book includes reproducible book pages for children to personalize with text and illustrations. Books feature traditional songs, fun rhymes, and predictable text to support emergent readers.

Book Links
On page 48, you'll find recommended picture books for each bookmaking activity to enrich learning. Share the picture books before completing the file-folder books to build children's interest and background knowledge, or use the books as an extension activity.

HOW TO MAKE FILE-FOLDER BOOKS

Getting Started

Before making books with students, gather the materials listed on the directions page. You might set up a writing center and keep a supply of bookmaking items organized in labeled plastic bins. Send home a letter to families requesting donations of supplies, such as fabric scraps, old magazines, ribbon, and so on.

Review the directions for a particular book project and determine which steps students will need assistance completing. Ask for parent volunteers to help in the bookmaking process.

Creating the Cover

Start with a colorful file folder, or sponge-paint a manila folder. Photocopy the cover template, preferably on card stock, and cut it out. Place the template on the front of the file folder (the scored lines should be facing up) with the straight edge of the template on the fold.

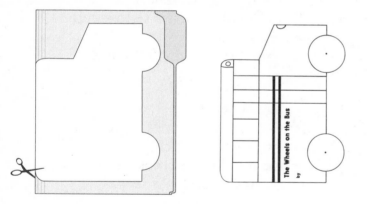

Trace the template and cut out the shape. Make sure to leave the fold on the file folder intact to become the book's spine. Open the cover on one of the scored lines. To create larger books, enlarge the cover template and interior book pages on your photocopying machine.

Children will need help cutting through the thickness of the front and back covers of the file folder. Invite parent volunteers to join you for a bookmaking session. Or you might ask parent volunteers to cut the folders at home. Decorate the cover any way you'd like—or use the ideas listed in the directions.

Safety Note: For added safety, round the edges.

Book-Making Basics

* file folders in assorted colors (available at office supply stores)
* lightweight card stock (available at office supply stores)
* copier paper
* construction paper
* tempera paint and brushes
* markers, crayons, and colored pencils
* safety scissors
* craft scissors (for adult use only)
* old magazines and catalogs
* stapler

Extra Goodies (optional)

* bright-colored copier paper or construction paper
* craft foam (plain and self-adhesive)
* white opaque markers (available at craft stores; great for drawing eyes or writing titles on dark paper)
* colorful dot stickers, labels, and name badges
* stickers
* rubber stamps and non-toxic washable dye ink pads
* glue gun (for adult use only)
* assorted art supplies such as ribbon, yarn, glitter, wiggly eyes, buttons, fake fur and fabric scraps, felt, and craft feathers

Creating the Inside Pages

Photocopy the book pages and cut them out along the solid lines. Refer to the directions for specific suggestions on completing each book. Here are additional suggestions:

- Have students complete the art and text before binding the pages together inside the cover.

- Have children write in pencil first, then check their work and have them trace their writing with thin marker.

- Before children begin writing, brainstorm possible responses to the prompts.

- Create charts of words and phrases for children to refer to as they write.

Binding the Books

Place the book pages in order and staple them to the inside back cover. For a fancier book, punch holes along the spine and bind the book with colorful ribbon, cord, yarn, or raffia. Your completed file-folder book is now ready to read and share!

Publishing Tips

- Keep extra blank file-folder books in the writing center for children to use.

- Adapt the directions and reproducibles to meet the needs of your students and curriculum.

- Invite children to make fun pointers to use as they read their finished books. Have them attach stickers or small objects to craft sticks. Glue or tape envelopes to the books' inside front covers and store the pointers inside.

- Use lightweight card stock instead of construction paper or poster board. It can be used in the copy machine, it's sturdy, and it's easier for little hands to cut than poster board.

- For instant repairs of errors that can't be erased, keep sheets of plain sticky labels handy. Just cover the error and keep on working!

- Save leftover file folder scraps to decorate other books (or to fix errors on the cover).

- Enlist the help of upper-grade buddies for cutting covers. High school students earning volunteer hours might be available before or after school.

- Invite children to add a "Meet the Author" page to the back cover.

Sharing the Books

Rereading text is an effective strategy for promoting fluency. Give children plenty of opportunities to interact with the text of each book before, during, and after making it. Here are some suggestions:

- Display the book's text in a pocket chart.

- Create a large collaborative class book or wall story with the book's text. Add children's illustrations.

- Place the completed file-folder books in your classroom library for independent reading.

- Read the completed books during small-group reading or guided reading time.

- Have children read their completed books with a classmate or upper-grade buddy.

- Have children store their completed books in empty cereal boxes that have been decorated.

- Send a note home to families offering suggestions for encouraging children to read their books, such as reading to family members or favorite stuffed animals, taking the books along to read in the dentist's waiting room, and having students glue a list to a book's inside back cover to keep track of all the people they've shared their book with.

The Wheels on the Bus

Create school bus books as a back-to-school activity, as part of a transportation unit, or as a response to a class field trip.

Follow these steps to create a class book, or help children create their own books.

1. Cut out the bus template. Place the top of the bus on the fold of the file folder and trace the template. Cut out the traced shape, leaving the fold of the file folder intact.

2. Cut out a wheel on the bus template. Trace it twice on black paper and cut out the shapes. Use brass fasteners to attach the wheels to the bus. (An adult should complete this step.)

3. Use markers and construction paper scraps to add windows and other details to the bus. Cut out pictures of students from your photocopied class photo, or cut out pictures of children from magazines. Glue the children in the bus windows. (As an alternative, draw children in the windows.) Write the title "The Wheels on the Bus."

4. Cut out the interior book pages. Arrange the pages in order and staple them to the inside back cover.

5. Have children fill in the blanks on the book pages with the missing words on each page. (page 1: *round and round*; *school*; page 2: *swish, swish, swish*; *school*; page 3: *beep, beep, beep*; *school*) If using the book as a response to a field trip, have children write the destination instead of the word *school*. On the last page, invite children to describe a real or imagined bus trip and their destination.

MORE WRITING

- Use the template to create a bus book with blank interior pages. Decorate the cover in a fanciful way with markers, stickers, stars, and so on, to design your own "magical" school bus. Read aloud a book from *The Magic School Bus* series by Joanna Cole (Scholastic) for inspiration. Then write a collaborative version of your class's own adventure.

- Write a collaborative class book about how students get to school each day. Invite each child to write and illustrate a page.

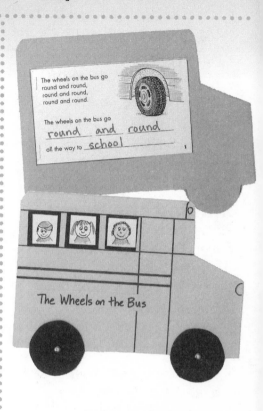

MATERIALS
for 1 book

* photocopies of cover template and book pages (pages 9–11)
* yellow file folder
* scissors
* black construction paper
* 2 brass paper fasteners
* construction paper scraps
* glue
* markers and crayons
* old magazines or photocopies of your class photo (optional)
* stapler

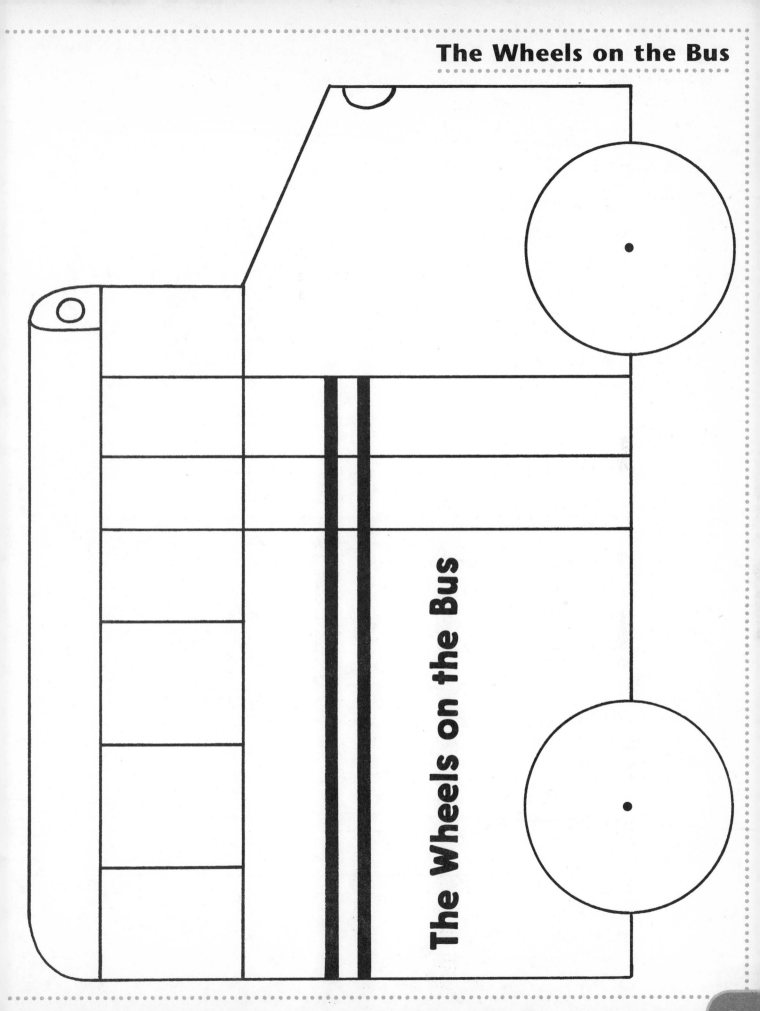

The Wheels on the Bus

The Wheels on the Bus

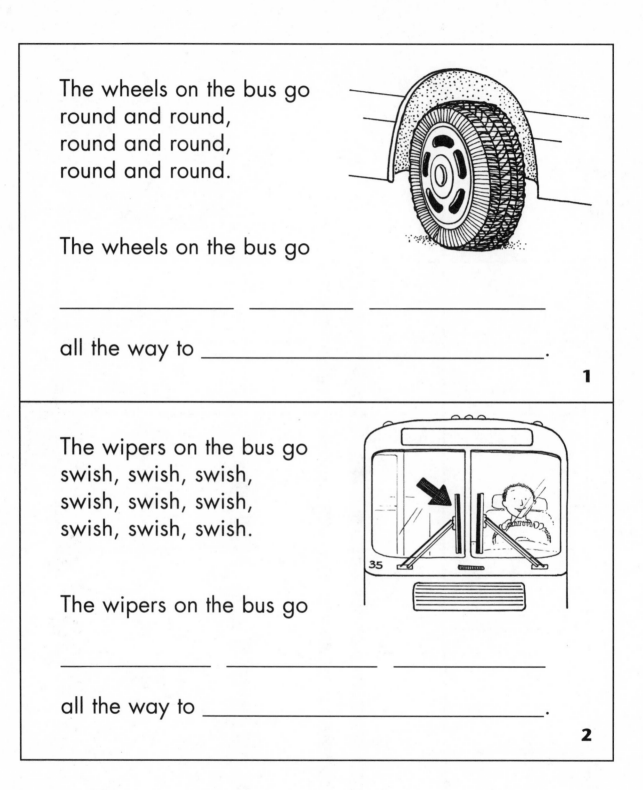

The wheels on the bus go
round and round,
round and round,
round and round.

The wheels on the bus go

_____ _____ _____

all the way to _____.

1

The wipers on the bus go
swish, swish, swish,
swish, swish, swish,
swish, swish, swish.

The wipers on the bus go

_____ _____ _____

all the way to _____.

2

The horn on the bus goes
beep, beep, beep,
beep, beep, beep,
beep, beep, beep.

The horn on the bus goes

_____ _____ _____

all the way to _____.

3

Where did the bus take you? Describe your trip.

_____

_____

_____

_____

_____

4

Silly Spiders

These spider books are great for Halloween, insect units, or anytime your class is ready for some creepy-crawly fun!

Follow these steps to create a class book, or help children create their own books.

1. Cut out the spider cover template. Place the top of the body on the fold of the file folder and trace the template. Cut out the traced shape, leaving the fold of the file folder intact.

2. Cut out the spider's head on the cover template. Trace the spider's head on purple paper and cut it out. Glue the head onto the cover.

3. Glue on wiggly eyes. Draw a smile and add the title "Silly Spiders."

4. Cut out the interior book pages. Arrange the pages in order and staple them to the inside back cover.

5. Have children color the illustrations on the book pages. Then have them fill in the blanks with the appropriate numbers and words (page 1: *4, web*; page 2: *3, tree*; page 3: *2, flower*; page 4: *1*). On page 4, have children draw a picture of themselves.

6. Optional: Punch a hole in the top of each book and hang the books from a spider web or tree in your reading corner.

MORE WRITING

- Cut out blank pages that are the same shape as the interior book pages. Create a collaborative book or have children add additional pages to their books following the pattern in the book. (I see ____ spiders. They are on the _____.) Invite children to illustrate each page to match the text.

- Use the templates to create a spider book with blank pages. Have children research spiders, then give them each a blank page on which to write and illustrate a spider fact. Compile the pages to create a nonfiction spider book.

MATERIALS
for 1 book

* photocopies of cover template and book pages (pages 13–15)
* brown file folder
* purple construction paper
* scissors
* glue
* 2 wiggly eyes
* thin black marker
* stapler
* markers and crayons
* hole punch and yarn (optional)

Silly Spiders

Silly Spiders

I see _____ silly spiders.

They are on the _____.

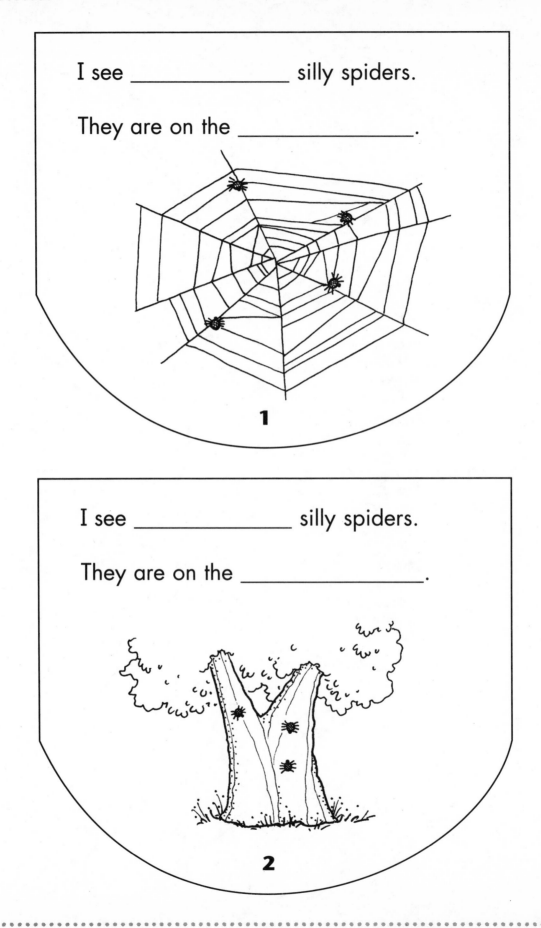

1

I see _____ silly spiders.

They are on the _____.

2

Super File-Folder Books   Scholastic Teaching Resources

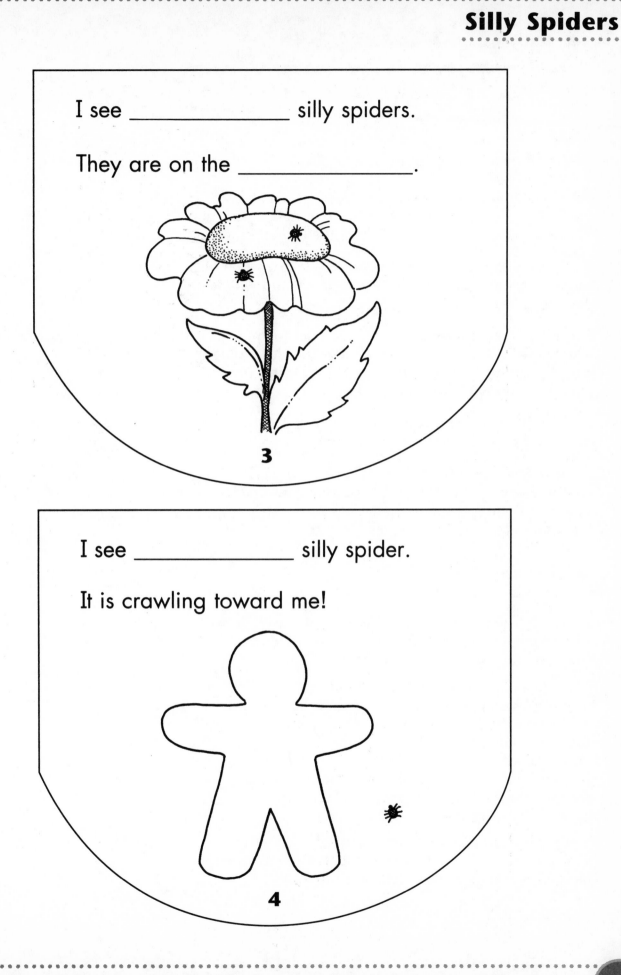

I see _____ silly spiders.

They are on the _____.

3

I see _____ silly spider.

It is crawling toward me!

4

I Like Books!

Celebrate reading with this project for Children's Book Week (the third week in November) or anytime!

Follow these steps to create a class book, or help children create their own books.

1. Cut out the book cover template. Place the spine on the fold of the file folder and trace the template. Cut out the traced shape, leaving the fold of the file folder intact.

2. Use markers to add details to the book. Attach a name badge label or small square of white paper, and write the title "I Like Books!"

3. Cut out a cute bookworm from green craft foam. Glue on wiggly eyes and draw other facial features. Either glue the worm onto the cover or glue it onto a craft stick for a fun pointer to use when reading the book.

4. Cut out the interior book pages. Arrange the pages in order and staple them to the inside back cover.

5. Invite children to color the illustrations on the first page. On the second page, have them fill in the lines with subjects of books, such as animals or sports. Encourage them to add illustrations to match the text.

MORE WRITING

• Add extra pages to the book using blank or lined paper. Have children write another verse to the poem or a paragraph describing their favorite book.

• The uses for this generic book cover are endless! Keep a supply of blank books in your writing center for children to use for book reports, journals, or for their own published stories. Use the book cover and blank pages to create ABC books, dictionaries, picture dictionaries, or journals. Or have children create another book that celebrates reading—for example, they can include pages showing whom they read to, who reads to them, where they read, and so on.

• Use the templates to create autobiography books with blank pages. Have children write information about themselves and glue their picture to the front.

MATERIALS
for 1 book

✳ photocopies of cover template and book pages (pages 17–19)

✳ red file folder (or any other color)

✳ scissors

✳ markers and crayons

✳ name badge labels or white construction paper scraps

✳ green craft foam

✳ 2 wiggly eyes

✳ glue

✳ craft stick (optional)

✳ stapler

I Like Books!

Do you like books about
airplanes, trucks, and cars?

Do you like books about
planets, space, and stars?

1

18

I like books about _____,
_____, and _____.
I like books about _____, too.

I like books about _____,
_____, and _____.
What kind of book can I read to you?

2

Miss Lucy

**Children can tote a purse-shaped book
to share this favorite song at home.**

**Follow these steps to create a class book,
or help children create their own books.**

1. Cut out the cover template. Place the feet on the fold of
   the file folder and trace the template. Cut out the traced
   shape, leaving the fold of the file folder intact. Cut out the
   inside of the handle on the front of the file folder. Then
   trace inside the space and cut out the shape on the back
   of the folder. (An adult should complete this step.)

2. Write the title "Miss Lucy" on the cover. Glue on wiggly
   eyes, as shown. Draw details such as facial features and
   bumps on the alligator's back. Cut teeth and toenails
   from the white paper and glue them to the alligator's
   mouth and feet (optional).

3. Cut out the interior book pages. Arrange the pages in
   order and staple them to the inside back cover.

4. Have students fill in the missing words on page 7
   (*doctor, nurse*) and page 8 (*lady*).

MORE WRITING

- Use the templates to create an alligator-purse book with
  blank pages for each student. (You might use lined paper
  for the interior pages.) Invite children to write about what
  else the lady with the alligator purse might keep in her bag.
  Have them write about one item on each page and add an
  illustration. For an extra challenge, ask children to think of
  objects that all begin with the letter *a* or another letter.
  Or, you might assign each student a different letter.

- Share picture books based on traditional songs, such as
  Miss Mary Mack by Mary Ann Hoberman (Little, Brown,
  1998) or *There Was an Old Lady Who Swallowed a Fly* by
  Simms Taback (Viking, 1997). Compare these renditions
  with the traditional songs. Are they different, similar, or
  the same? Invite children to choose their favorite verse
  and draw an illustration to match, then compile the pages
  into a collaborative class book.

MATERIALS
for 1 book

- ✳ photocopies of cover template
  and book pages (pages 21–23)
- ✳ green file folder
- ✳ scissors
- ✳ thin black marker
- ✳ 2 wiggly eyes
- ✳ glue
- ✳ scraps of white construction paper
  or craft foam (optional)
- ✳ stapler

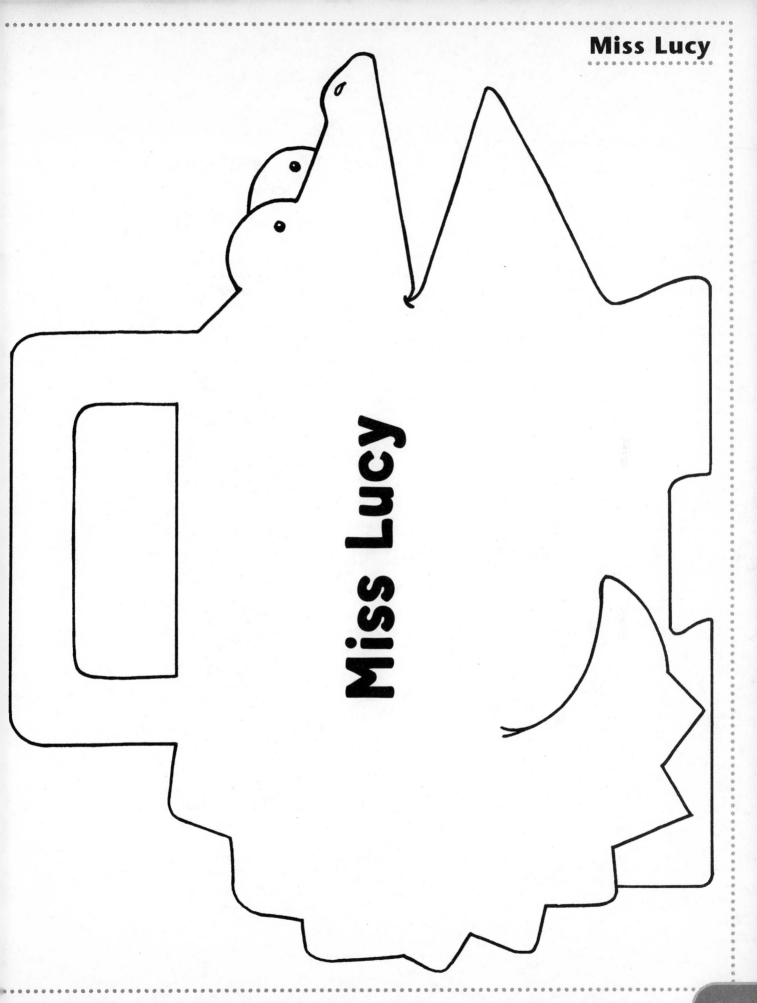

Miss Lucy

Miss Lucy had a turtle.
His name was Tiny Tim.

1

She put him in the bathtub
to see if he could swim.

2

He drank up all the water.
He ate up all the soap.

3

He tried to eat the bathtub,
but it wouldn't go down his throat.

4

Miss Lucy called the doctor.
Miss Lucy called the nurse.

5

Miss Lucy called the lady
with the alligator purse.

6

"Mumps," said the _____.

"Measles," said the _____.

7

"Nonsense!" said the _____
with the alligator purse.

8

Ten Little Dinosaurs

This "dino-mite" subtraction story will liven up any math lesson!

Follow these steps to create a class book, or help children create their own books.

1. Cut out the dinosaur cover template. Place the feet on the fold of the file folder and trace the template. Cut out the traced shape, leaving the fold of the file folder intact.

2. Write the title "Ten Little Dinosaurs" on the cover. Draw details on the dinosaur, such as facial features and a line on its back. Attach wiggly eyes and dot stickers or paper circles for spots.

3. Cut out the interior book pages. Add art to page 1 (gate), page 2 (tree), and page 3 (sun).

4. Arrange the pages in order and staple them to the inside back cover.

5. Photocopy, cut out, and color the dinosaur manipulatives. For greater durability, glue them onto small squares of construction paper. Or you might create the manipulatives with rubber stamps or stickers of dinosaurs. Store the manipulatives in a plastic bag and staple it to the back cover.

6. Have students fill in the blanks on the book pages with the appropriate numbers. Show them how to use the dinosaur manipulatives to help them solve the math problems. Then have students fill in the subtraction equation at the bottom of each page.

MORE WRITING

- Read aloud *How Do Dinosaurs Say Goodnight?* by Jane Yolen (Scholastic, 2000). Have children write a "how-to" book with the steps they would take to get a lively dinosaur to bed at night.

- Use the templates to create a dinosaur book with blank interior pages. On the first page, write the rhyme:
    Here is a dinosaur I just met.
    I hope it can be my pet.
  Ask children to finish the story by writing about how they would take care of their new pet. On the cover, add a title such as "My New Pet."

MATERIALS
for 1 book

* photocopies of cover template and book pages (pages 25–27)

* green file folder (or any other color)

* scissors

* thin black marker

* 2 wiggly eyes

* glue

* 5 dot stickers or small paper circles (different color than file folder)

* stapler

* 10 dinosaur manipulatives (pages 26–27)

* colored construction paper scraps

* small, resealable plastic bag

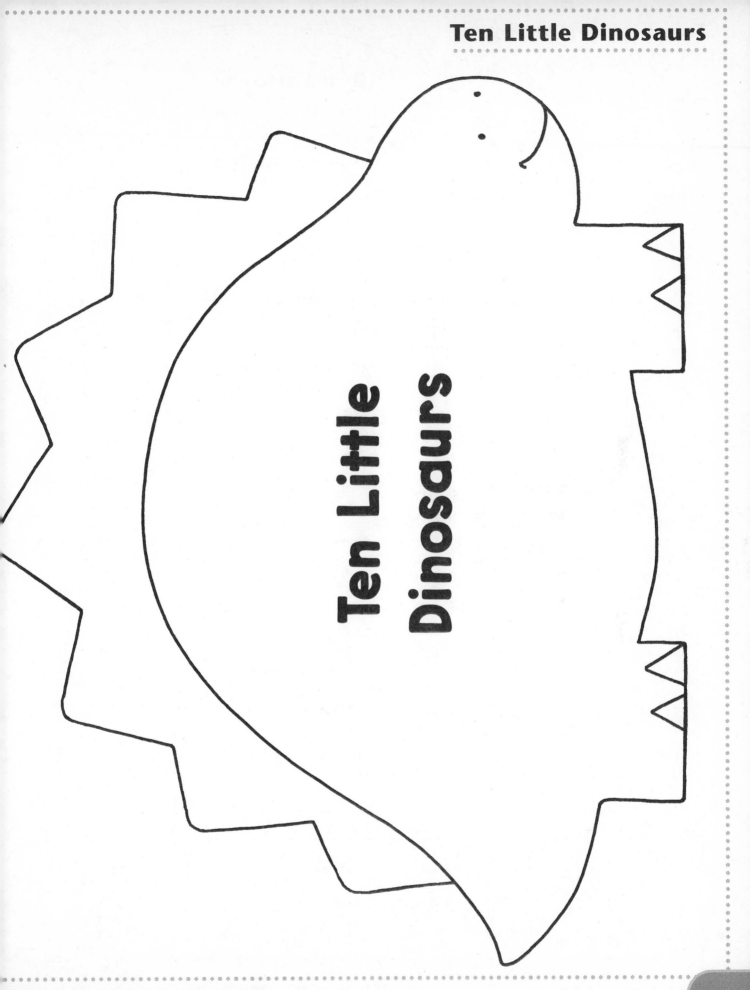

Ten Little Dinosaurs

Ten Little Dinosaurs

10 little dinosaurs
playing by the gate.
2 ran away
and now there are _____.

[ ] − [ ] = [ ]

1

8 little dinosaurs
playing by the tree.
5 ran away
and now there are _____.

[ ] − [ ] = [ ]

2

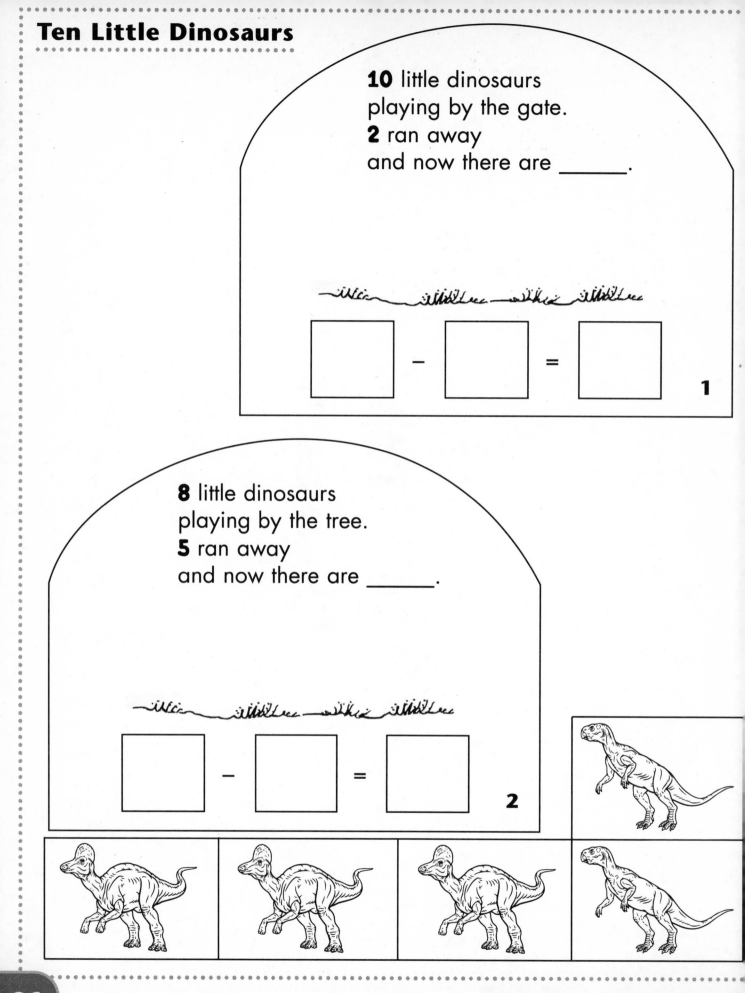

Super File-Folder Books   Scholastic Teaching Resources

3 little dinosaurs
playing in the sun.
2 ran away
and now there is _____.

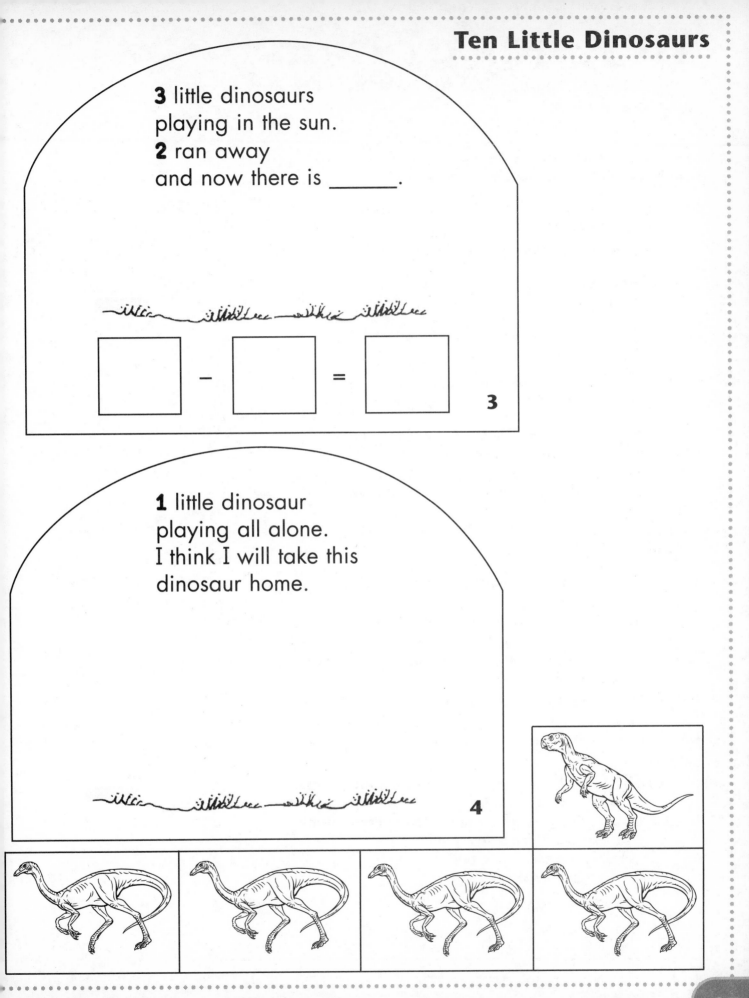

☐ − ☐ = ☐

3

1 little dinosaur
playing all alone.
I think I will take this
dinosaur home.

4

All Kinds of Homes

Explore animal homes with this textured nest-shaped book.

Follow these steps to create a class book, or help children create their own books.

1. Cut out the nest cover template. Place the bottom of the nest on the fold of the file folder and trace the template. Cut out the traced shape, leaving the fold of the file folder intact.

2. Draw details on the nest and write the title "All Kinds of Homes."

3. Cut eggs from white paper scraps and glue them in the nest.

4. Cut out the interior book pages. Arrange the pages in order and staple them to the inside back cover.

5. Show students how to fill in the blanks with the appropriate animal names (1—*bird*, 2—*bear*, 3—*spider*, 4—*bee*, 5—*beaver*). On the last page, instruct students to draw lines to match the animals with their homes.

MORE WRITING

- Read *The Big Orange Splot* by Daniel Pinkwater (Hastings House, 1977). Invite children to draw a home that looks "like your dreams," just as Mr. Plumbean did. Encourage them to be creative in their designs. Invite children to write a description of their dream home to go with their illustration.

- Use the templates to create a nest book with blank interior pages. Have children research birds that build different kinds of nests. They might include penguins, cliff swallows, and weaverbirds.

- Read aloud *A House Is a House for Me* by Mary Ann Hoberman (Viking, 1978). Then ask children to write their own poem about animal homes using the same frame. For example:

  An anthill is a home for an ant.
  A cave is a home for a bat.
  A web is a home for a spider,
  But a _____ is a home for me!

MATERIALS
for 1 book

- ✴ photocopies of cover template and book pages (pages 29–31)
- ✴ yellow or tan file folder
- ✴ scissors
- ✴ thin marker
- ✴ white construction paper scraps
- ✴ raffia
- ✴ glue
- ✴ stapler

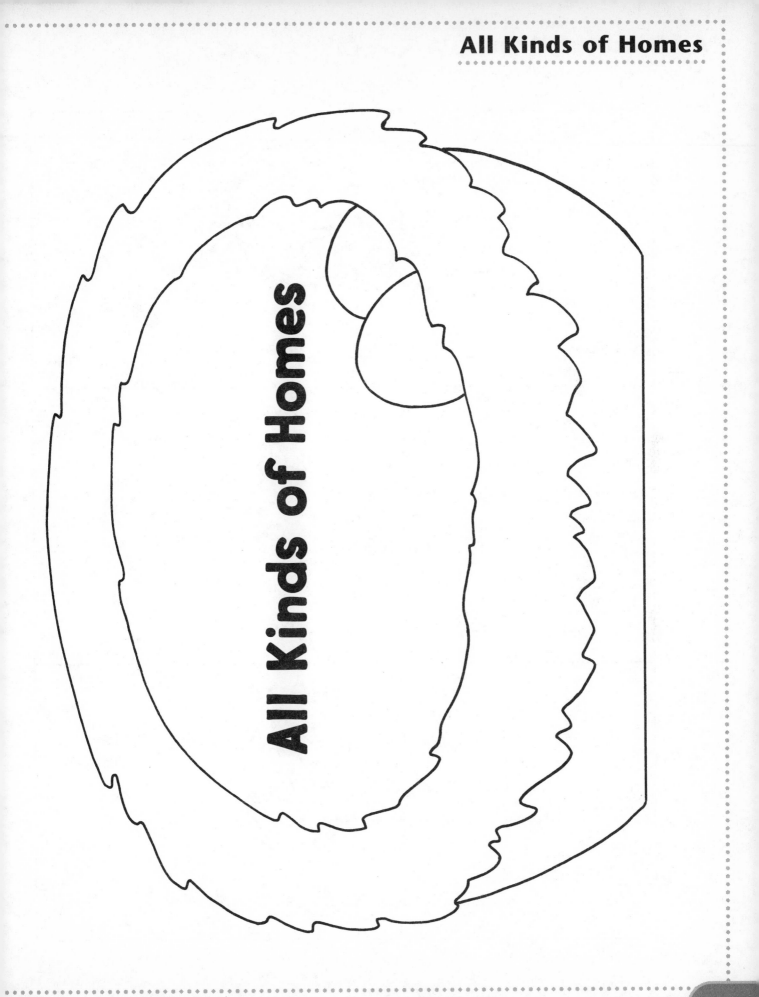

All Kinds of Homes

All Kinds of Homes

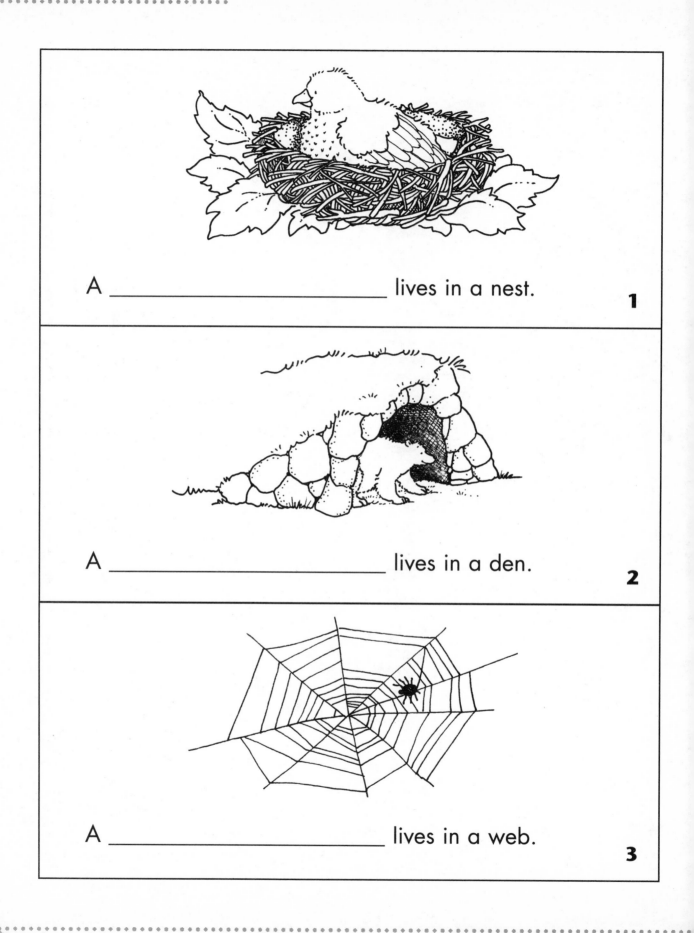

A _____ lives in a nest.

1

A _____ lives in a den.

2

A _____ lives in a web.

3

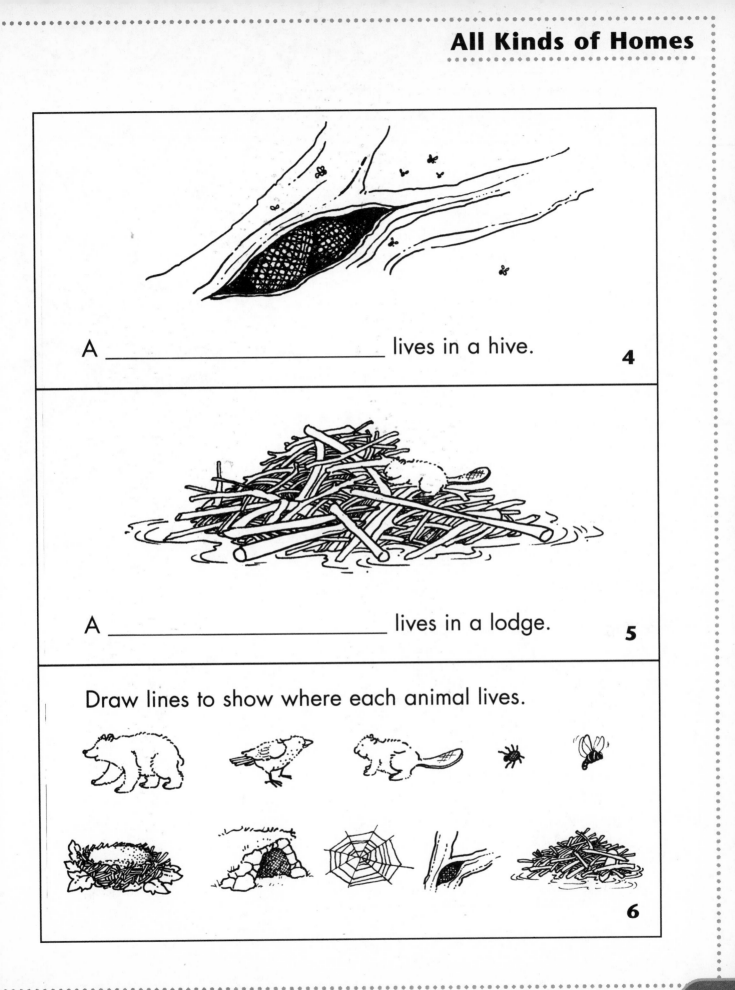

A _____ lives in a hive.

4

A _____ lives in a lodge.

5

Draw lines to show where each animal lives.

6

My Monster Book

Children use their imaginations to create a fun-filled book with an adorable, textured cover.

Follow these steps to create a class book, or help children create their own books.

1. Cut out the monster cover template. Place the top of the monster on the fold of the file folder and trace the template. Cut out the traced shape, leaving the fold of the file folder intact.

2. Glue on wiggly eyes. Use a black marker to draw the tail and head. Write the title "My Monster Book."

3. Draw other details such as facial features, toenails, and teeth. Cut shapes from paper scraps, felt, and fake fur and glue them onto the monster for colorful decoration.

4. Cut out the interior book pages. Arrange the pages in order and staple them to the inside back cover.

5. Have children fill in the blanks on the book pages by writing something that playful, silly monsters might like. Invite them to draw pictures to match the text. Or, provide a variety of small objects for students to glue onto the pages.

MORE WRITING

- Invite children to imagine a fun, adorable monster they might want as a pet. Have them write a description of their monster and how they would take care of it. Ask them to think about the following questions:

    What does your monster look like?
    What kind of noise does it make?
    What does it eat?
    Where does it sleep?
    What does it like to do?
    What do you do to take good care of your pet?

- Read aloud *Five Ugly Monsters* by Tedd Arnold (Scholastic, 1995). Have children write their own version using this book as a model.

MATERIALS
for 1 book

* photocopies of cover template and book pages (pages 33–35)

* purple file folder (or any other color)

* scissors

* wiggly eyes

* glue

* thin black marker

* felt or fake fur scraps

* craft foam and construction paper scraps

* stapler

My Monster Book

My Monster Book

Some monsters like _____. **1**

Some monsters like _____. **2**

Some monsters like _____. **3**

Some monsters like _____. 4

Some monsters like _____. 5

But all monsters like _____! 6

Button Bear

Children make an adorable bear-shaped book featuring words that begin with the letter _b_.

Follow these steps to create a class book, or help children create their own books.

1. Cut out the bear cover template. Place the left side of the bear on the fold of the file folder and trace the template. Cut out the traced shape, leaving the fold of the file folder intact.

2. Glue on wiggly eyes and two or three buttons. For a fun pointer, glue a button onto a craft stick and use it when reading the text.

3. Draw facial features and other details. Write the title "Button Bear."

4. To add some texture, cut out circles from craft foam and glue them onto the bear's ears and feet. Glue a bow onto the bear's head or neck. (Both steps are optional.)

5. Cut out the interior book pages. Arrange the pages in order and staple them to the inside back cover.

6. Have children fill in the blanks on the book pages with objects that begin with _b_. Then have them illustrate each sentence.

MORE WRITING

- Adopt a traveling class bear! Have children take turns bringing home a stuffed bear with an accompanying journal. Invite them to write about an activity they shared with the bear and add an illustration.

- Together, sing the traditional jump rope song "Teddy Bear." Then invite children to write their own versions, featuring their favorite bear. For example:
  Huggy Bear, Huggy Bear! Tie your shoe.
  Huggy Bear, Huggy Bear! I love you!

- Use bear stickers or bear stamp art to create a book titled, "Where Is My Bear?" Feature different position words on each page. For example,
  Where is my bear? My bear is beside my bed.
  Where is my bear? My bear is in my bed.
  Where is my bear? My bear is under my bed.

MATERIALS
for 1 book

- ✳ photocopies of cover template and book pages (pages 37–39)
- ✳ blue file folder (or any other color)
- ✳ scissors
- ✳ thin marker
- ✳ 2 wiggly eyes
- ✳ 2–4 colorful buttons
- ✳ glue
- ✳ markers
- ✳ pink or white craft foam scraps (optional)
- ✳ ribbon scraps (optional)
- ✳ craft stick (optional)
- ✳ stapler

Button
Bear

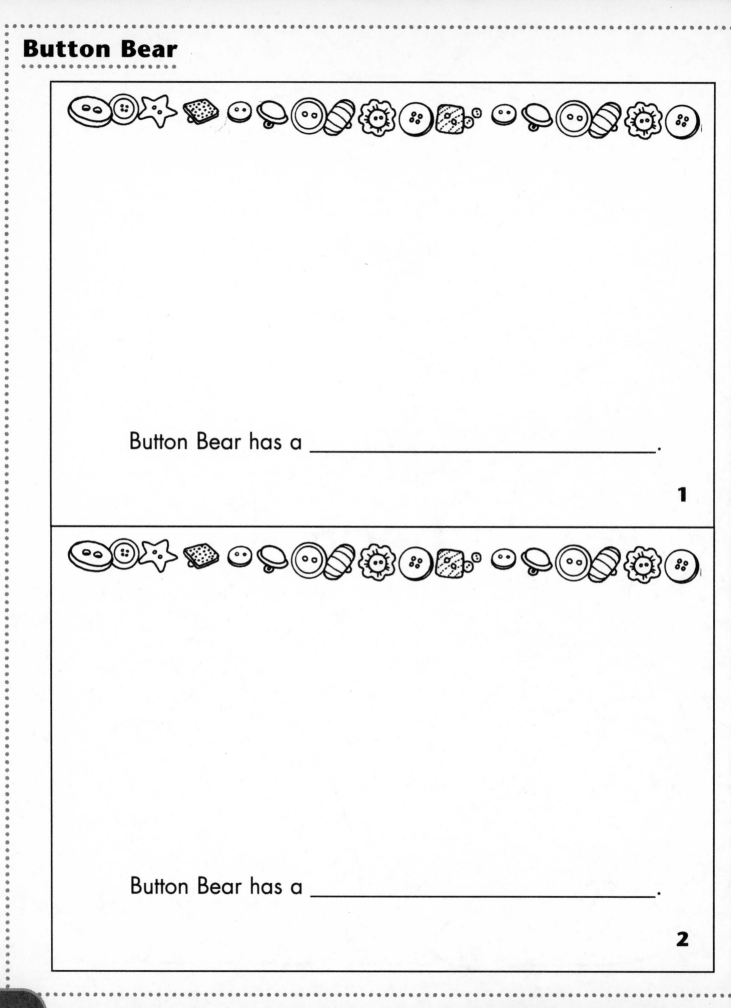

Button Bear has a _____.

1

Button Bear has a _____.

2

Button Bear has a _____.

3

Button Bear has a _____ just for me!

4

Piggy Bank Book

A piggy bank book with manipulatives helps children learn coin values!

Follow these steps to create a class book, or help children create their own books.

1. Cut out the pig cover template. Place the top of the pig on the fold of the file folder and trace the template. Cut out the traced shape, leaving the fold of the file folder intact.

2. Glue on wiggly eyes and a button nose. (If a button is unavailable, cut a circle from construction paper or craft foam.) Cut out ears from craft foam and glue them onto the pig. Glue on a curlicue tail fashioned from a pipe cleaner. Use a black marker to draw other details, such as eyelashes, a mouth, and a 2 1/8-inch straight line for a coin slot.

3. Cut out the interior book pages. Arrange the pages in order and staple them to the inside back cover.

4. Photocopy and cut out the coin manipulatives. Have children glue the appropriate coins in the boxes on the book pages and write the coin values. On the last page, ask them to choose a combination of coin manipulatives and glue them onto the page. Then have children write which coins they chose (a *penny and 2 nickels*, and so on) and the total number of cents.

5. To extend learning, create coin strips to use with the book. Carefully cut a coin slit in the cover. (An adult should complete this step.) Cut strips from card stock approximately 2- by 8- inches in size. At the top of the strip, glue several coin manipulatives. Turn the strip over and write the equivalent money amount. Show students how to insert the strip into the slot so that all the coins show at the top. Have them determine the money amount, then pull the strip through and check the answer on the back. Store the strips in a plastic bag attached to the back cover of the book.

MORE WRITING

• Use the templates to create a pig book with blank pages. Invite students to research and write about pigs and other farm animals to create a nonfiction book.

MATERIALS
for 1 book

* photocopies of cover template and book pages (pages 41–43)

* pink file folder (or manila folder painted pink)

* scissors

* 2 wiggly eyes

* large pink or red button (optional)

* pink or red craft foam scraps

* glue

* thin black marker

* pink or red pipe cleaner, cut into a 3-inch piece with sharp ends folded in

* stapler

* crayons

* coin manipulatives

* card stock (optional)

* gallon-size resealable plastic bag and stapler (optional)

Piggy Bank Book

Piggy Bank Book

I have a nickel. Yes, I do.

I have _____ cents just for you!

1

I have a dime. Yes, I do.

I have _____ cents just for you!

2

Super File-Folder Books   Scholastic Teaching Resources

I have a quarter. Yes, I do.

I have _____ cents just for you!

3

I have _____. Yes, I do.

I have _____ cents just for you!

4

On the Go!

Children write about what they'll pack for a real or imaginary trip in this travel-themed book.

Follow these steps to create a class book, or help children create their own books.

1. Cut out the suitcase cover template. Place the handle of the suitcase on the fold of the file folder and trace the template. Cut out the traced shape, leaving the fold of the file folder intact. Cut out the inside of the handle on the front of the file folder. Then trace inside the space and cut out the shape on the back of the folder. (An adult should complete this step.)

2. Write the title "On the Go!" on the cover. Decorate the suitcase with pictures of various destinations, using markers, pictures cut from travel brochures, or travel-themed stickers. Or you might draw pictures on plain self-adhesive labels to create your own travel stickers.

3. Cut out a luggage tag from an index card, punch a hole in it, and attach it to the suitcase handle with a piece of yarn, cord, or a key chain. If creating individual books for students, have students write their name on the tag.

4. Cut out the interior book pages. Arrange the pages in order and staple them to the inside back cover.

5. Have students fill in the blanks on the book pages with objects to pack for a real or imaginary trip. Invite them to add illustrations or glue pictures cut from magazines or catalogs.

MORE WRITING

• Invite students to create a school vacation journal. Have them write about their special trips or experiences. Encourage them to include drawings, photos, postcards, stickers, and other memorabilia.

MATERIALS
for 1 book

* photocopies of cover template and book pages (pages 45–47)
* red file folder (or any other color)
* scissors
* markers and crayons
* travel-themed stickers or blank adhesive labels (optional)
* travel catalogs or brochures (optional)
* glue
* hole punch
* index cards
* yarn, cord, or small key chains
* old magazines or catalogs
* stapler

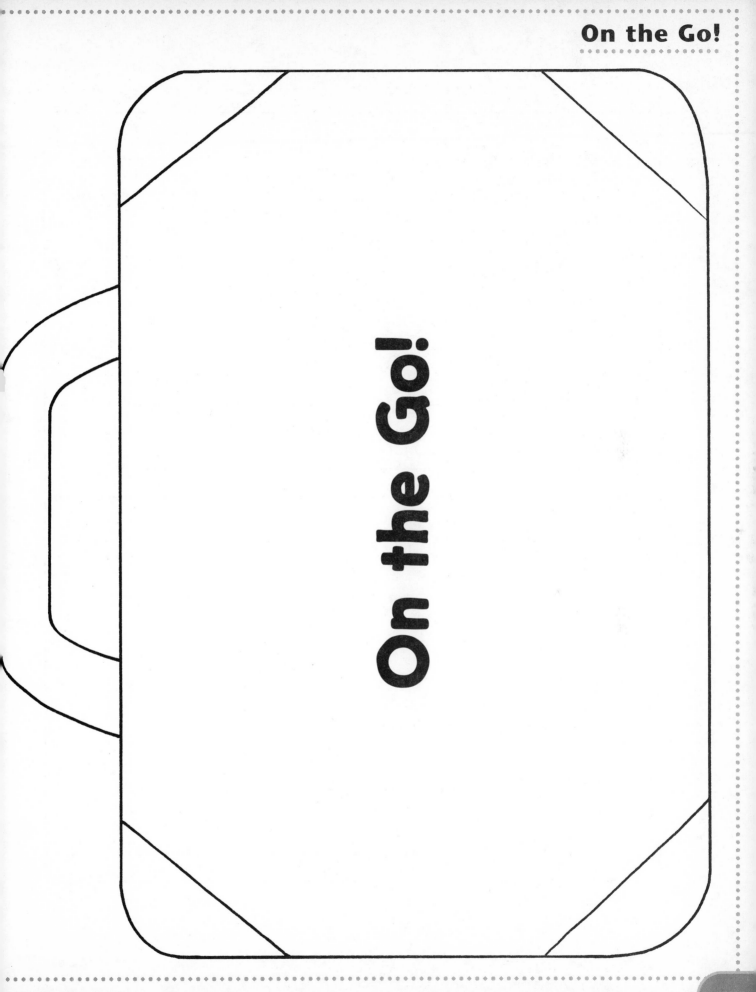

On the Go!

I will pack my _____.

I will pack my _____. **1**

I will pack my _____.

I will pack my _____. **2**

I will pack my _____.

I will pack my _____. **3**

I will pack my _____.

I am going to _____! **4**

BOOK LINKS
Share these read-alouds to build children's interest, vocabulary, and background knowledge.

The Wheels on the Bus
This Is the Way We Go to School
by Edith Baer (Scholastic, 1990)
Readers learn how children all
over the world travel to school.

The Wheels on the Bus by Maryann
Kovalski (Joy Street Books, 1987)
Grandma and children sing this
familiar song so enthusiastically
that they miss their bus.

Silly Spiders
Spiders, Spiders Everywhere!
by Rozanne Lanczak Williams
(Creative Teaching Press, 1995)
Spiders and poetry come together
in an engaging story that teaches
young readers about numbers.

Spiders Spin Webs by Yvonne
Winer (Charlesbridge, 1996)
This book features poems and
exquisite illustrations about
spiders spinning webs.

I Like Books!
Good Books, Good Times!
by Lee Bennett Hopkins
(HarperCollins, 1990)
Readers celebrate the magic
of reading with this fun-filled
collection of poetry.

Wolf! by Becky Bloom
(Orchard Books, 1999)
Wolf decides to learn to read in
order to impress the farm animals.

Miss Lucy
Counting Crocodiles by Judy
Sierra (Harcourt Brace, 1997)
How does a clever monkey reach
the banana tree on a distant island?
Readers will be delighted to find out.

The Lady With the Alligator Purse
adapted and illustrated by Nadine
Bernard Westcott
(Little, Brown & Company, 1988)
This book presents a playful
adaptation of the traditional song.

Ten Little Dinosaurs
Danny and the Dinosaur
by Syd Hoff (Harper Trophy, 1993)
A boy visits a museum and
makes a surprising friend.

How Do Dinosaurs Say Good Night?
by Jane Yolen (Blue Sky Press, 2000)
Mother and children guess how
dinosaurs might have said
good night.

All Kinds of Homes
The Big Orange Splot
by Daniel Manus Pinkwater
(Hasting House, 1977)
A seagull drops a can of orange
paint on a house and gives
the owner a clever idea.

A House Is a House for Me
by Mary Ann Hoberman
(Viking Press, 1978)
Rhyming, rhythmic text describes
a wide variety of homes.

My Monster Book
Huggly series by Tedd Arnold
(Scholastic, 1997)
A friendly monster from under
the bed embarks upon various
adventures.

The Purple Snerd
by Rozanne Lanczak Williams
(Harcourt, 2000)
Fern makes an unusual friend
in this humorous tale.

Button Bear
Ira Sleeps Over by Bernard Waber
(Houghton Mifflin, 1972)
Ira worries about his first sleepover
and wonders whether he
should take his teddy bear.

Where's My Teddy?
by Jez Alborough
(Candlewick, 1992)
Eddie searches the forest for his
lost teddy and finds a real bear
with the same problem.

The Piggy Bank Book
The Coin Counting Book
by Rozanne Lanczak Williams
(Charlesbridge, 2001)
Rhymes and photographs
introduce coins to young learners.

Jelly Beans for Sale
by Bruce McMillan
(Scholastic, 1996)
Children learn about coin
values in an engaging book
about buying jelly beans.

On the Go!
*How to Make an Apple Pie and See
the World* by Marjorie Priceman
(Random House, 1996)
Shopping for groceries leads to
world travel and exploration.

Stringbean's Trip to the Shining Sea
by Vera B. Williams and Jennifer
Williams (Greenwillow, 1988)
A collection of postcards describes
a cross-country trip.

Super File-Folder Books   Scholastic Teaching Resources